meditations

for new parents

THE CLASSIC BESTSELLING SERIES

meditations
for new parents

A book of inspiration for new parents

Revised Edition

GERALD SHENK *and*
SARA WENGER SHENK

Herald Press

Harrisonburg, Virginia
Kitchener, Ontario

Library of Congress has cataloged the original edition as follows:
Shenk, Gerald, 1953-
    Meditations for new parents / Gerald and Sara Wenger Shenk.
        p. cm.
    ISBN 0-8361-9038-6 (alk. paper) 1. Parents—Prayer-books and devo-
tions—English. 2. Parenting—Religious aspects—Christianity—Meditations.
3. Devotional calendars. I. Shenk, Sara Wenger, 1953- . II. Title.
BV4845.S48 1996
242'.645—dc20

                                        95-48808

MEDITATIONS FOR NEW PARENTS
© 1996, 2004, 2014 by Herald Press,
Harrisonburg, Virginia 22802
    Released simultaneously in Canada by Herald Press,
    Kitchener, Ontario N2G 3R1. All rights reserved.
First edition 1996. Second edition 2004. Third edition 2014.
Library of Congress Catalog Card Number: 95-48808
International Standard Book Number: 978-0-8361-9038-0
Printed in the United States of America
Design by Reuben Graham

Unless otherwise indicated, Scripture quotations are from the *New Revised
Standard Version Bible*, © 1989, by the Division of Christian Education
of the National Council of the Churches of Christ in the USA, and used by
permission.

To order or request information please call 1-800-245-7894 or visit
www.heraldpress.com.

18 17 16 15 14   9 8 7 6 5

To Joseph,
Timothy, and Greta;
dearest companions
on the journey

Contents

· · · · · · · · · · · · · · · · ·

A Parenting God

. . . .

Preface

. . . .

Welcome to an adventure unlike any you've been on. No matter who has gone this way before you, now is your time for an appointment with the destiny of parenthood. Each story is unique. Yours begins now—and will continue forever.

The newborn baby demands and deserves a lot of attention. And as new parents, you too need support and affirmation. This is a vulnerable, formative time for you and your child alike.

Through this collection of meditations, we want to walk with you into some moments of reflection on the awesome prospects ahead. We hope someone was kind enough to give you this book as a gesture of support. Perhaps they also know how precious it is to find rare moments for spiritual nurture during the first days and weeks of parenting a newborn child.

This companion for your spiritual journey will be used best if you as parents can work with it together. It is intended to strengthen your unity as partners in the venture, to ground you in the wisdom of the generations before us. Most of all, these reflections are designed to nurture your spirits, reconnecting you with the One who made us all. You are not alone!

May God be your strength by day, and your song in the night.

Gerald and Sara

. . . .

WELCOME STRANGER

. . . .

Whoever welcomes one such
child in my name welcomes me.

—Matthew 18:5

. . . .

The Fruit of Our Love

. . . .

Therefore a man leaves his father and his mother and clings to his wife, and they become one flesh. And the man and his wife were both naked, and were not ashamed.

—Genesis 2:24-25

Set me as a seal upon your heart, as a seal upon your arm; for love is strong as death, passion fierce as the grave. Its flashes are flashes of fire, a raging flame. Many waters cannot quench love, neither can floods drown it. If one offered for love all the wealth of his house, it would be utterly scorned" (Song of Solomon 8:6-7).

There is a mystery that confounds even the most probing minds—a man and woman in love; and not only in love today, but for better or worse until death. Oh, there is much sham love that masquerades, pretending to deliver the goods. But it utterly fails. It is those who are naked even to the depths of their souls and still unashamed who know the joy of total abandonment in the embrace of their beloved.

The mystery of becoming one flesh only deepens with time. The Spirit of God intermingles with our spirits, weaving a love bond that is unparalleled in its texture and richness. And in God's design, a new life is conceived within the weaving of that cradle of intimate tenderness. In that most private, passionate knowing of one other, an unfathomable choreography of creation is set into motion.

The fruit of our love leads us into the mystery and complexity of God's being. As new parents we are drawn slowly but surely into the Creator's delightful dance of life, stepping to the music of heaven come to earth.

Holy One, we are humbled by the way you have included us in your dance. We grow dizzy and breathless with its beauty and complexity. How can we respond except to bow down with gratitude and worship? Amen.

PRAYER

"To pray is to take notice of the wonder, to regain a sense of the mystery that animates all beings, the divine margin in all attainments." Prayer is "our" humble "answer" to the inconceivable surprise of living. It is all we can offer in return for the mystery by which we live. Who is worthy to be present at the constant unfolding of time? Amidst the meditation of mountains, the humility of flowers—wiser than all alphabets—clouds that die constantly for the sake of His glory, "we" are hating, hunting, hurting. Suddenly we feel ashamed for our clashes and complaints in the face of the tacit glory in nature. It is so embarrassing to live! How strange we are in the world, and how presumptuous our doings! Only one response can maintain us: gratefulness for witnessing the wonder, for the gift of our unearned right to serve, to adore, and to fulfill. It is gratefulness which makes the soul great.

—*Abraham Joshua Heschel*,
Man's Quest for God

. . . .

Intimate Stranger

. . . .

For it was you who formed my inward parts; you knit me together in my mother's womb. . . . My frame was not hidden from you, when I was being made in secret, intricately woven in the depths of the earth.

—Psalm 139:13, 15

While carrying our unborn baby, Sara was amused by how little she needed to do to shape this new being into *being*. She wrote a friend, "As the systems and limbs are invisibly knit together, we wonder in awe and await with joy the unveiling." As with Samuel's mother, Ruth's mother, Jesus' mother, and every other mother, she simply ate, slept, and pursued her work while the most amazing processes of creation were unfolding within. A new life that hadn't existed before would now *be* throughout all eternity.

Months ticked slowly by as the baby pushed more and more into the space between us. This little being will not dissolve, we mused. There *will* be a birth. A birth or a death. Stark alternatives. Inescapable. Inevitable. We were embarking on an exhilarating, sometimes frightening adventure with another human being who was both a part of us and yet not us, who was more and more present with us and yet cloaked in mystery. An intimate stranger—so close and yet so unknown.

Where would it all end? Never! We together had initiated another "message to the future," as Michael Novak said, "carried in relays generation after generation, carried since the dim beginnings." Our little intimate would be another link in a great chain of being that stretches through the ages, forever. Our hearts shuddered with fear and anticipation. Did we have the resources to handle the unveiling of our intimate stranger? Would there be joy or numb disappointment? Along with many other new parents, we prayed and waited.

Good Shepherd, on the threshold of this new responsibility we are afraid. Are we ready? What will be required of us? Tender Shepherd, be our constant companion as we venture into the unknown. Amen.

(*AT*, pp. 28, 30)

THE LAMB

Little Lamb, who made thee?
Dost thou know who made thee?
Gave thee life, and bid thee feed
By the stream and o'er the mead;
Gave thee clothing of delight,
Softest clothing, wooly, bright;
Gave thee such a tender voice,
Making all the vales rejoice?
Little Lamb, who made thee?
Dost thou know who made thee?

Little Lamb, I'll tell thee,
Little Lamb, I'll tell thee:
He is called by thy name,
For he calls himself a Lamb.
He is meek, and he is mild;
He became a little child.
I a child, and thou a lamb,
We are called by his name.
Little Lamb, God bless thee!
Little Lamb, God bless thee!

—*William Blake*, Songs of Innocence

. . . .

Womb-Love

. . . .

Yet it was you who took me from the womb, you kept me safe on my mother's breast. On you I was cast from my birth, and since my mother bore me you have been my God.

—Psalm 22:9-10

Conceiving, birthing, and raising children is commonplace, is it not?

Indeed it is! But you can talk with such nonchalance only until *you* are pregnant; until *your* automatic systems go into gear to produce another unique embodiment of God's image; until *you*, somebody's child, become overnight, somebody's parent. To give birth is at once very everyday and absolutely profound. Its impact is very personal and deeply felt.

"All human life on the planet is born of woman," writes Adrienne Rich in her book *Of Woman Born*. The one unifying experience shared by all men and all women is that months-long period inside a woman's body while we were formed. And every person, whether pauper or princess, was at one time nourished as a helpless infant by someone who at least minimally cared.

God is portrayed in Scripture in some profoundly maternal ways. The Hebrew word for God's compassion includes the meaning of "womb-love." Whenever we read about God's compassion for us, we can think of God carrying us as a mother tenderly carries her unborn child. Womb-love is intimate and all-encompassing.

As Sara carried our unborn child, there was hardly a moment when she wasn't conscious of the tiny person within. We were continually concerned that all would be well. We knew that though this was an experience familiar to so many, *we* had never felt so vulnerable before. We took great comfort in knowing that God's compassion surrounded us as new parents with vigilance and tenderness, much like a mother's womb encircles a fledgling fetus.

Encircle us, gentle Protector, with your sturdy arms. Surround us with your vigilant watchfulness. It is your tender loving care that gives us the courage to put protecting arms around our own child. Amen.

(*AT*, pp. 26, 27)

PARENTHOOD

Marriage is, then, very much a spiritual journey. So also is its most extraordinary result, parenthood.

To become a parent is to form the most intimate of all covenants with God. Abraham's original covenant with God was first of all a promise that he and Sarah would have a child; everything else followed upon this. And so too the new covenant, begun when the angel appeared to Mary and later to Joseph and announced the coming birth of Jesus. Both couples, Abraham and Sarah and Mary and Joseph, were given essentially the same message: first, that they were to have a child, and, second, that through their relationship with this child their relationship to God would deepen profoundly.

In this the births of Isaac and Jesus are identical to that of every child. With each baby born a private, intensely personal bond is formed between the parents and God, one weighted with burdens, and also with quiet gifts. . . .

All the lessons of parenthood spring from the hard work of loving. I have often suspected that all that occurs in childhood, all the awkwardness of the adolescent years, all the delicate maturation of early adulthood—all of that apparent growth is just the climbing of the stairs to the schoolhouse door. It is with parenthood that the door is opened; it is then the lessons begin.

—*Ernest Boyer Jr.*, Finding God at Home[1]

. . . .

Bringing Forth Life

. . . .

When a woman is in labor, she has pain, because her hour has come. But when her child is born, she no longer remembers the anguish because of the joy of having brought a human being into the world.

—John 16:21

Birthing a baby together can be an unsurpassed highlight for new parents. When modern medicine, to the best of its ability, ensures a safe delivery and stands by supportively, mother and father can labor together. The grand climax of birth then is wondrous—beyond description. Words fail us in that moment of pure joy. Instead, as we hold our little intimate, no longer stranger, in our arms for the first time, tears of profound gratitude well up.

We experienced the goodness of the Giver, but not as we anticipated. Not all births are glorious events. Our first one was laced with complications and frightening emergency interventions. But mercifully, in our helplessness we were borne up by the Good Shepherd and carried into parenthood on his sturdy arms.

Despite the trauma, it was with tears of relief that Sara first nestled our son against her breast some two days after delivery. And after eleven days, we both walked out of the hospital with our baby finally in our charge. On a bitterly cold, white day in January, Gerald gingerly carried our warm bundle over icy sidewalks and steps to his first real home. At long last we could touch, caress, ogle, and gloat to our hearts' content.

Long forgotten lullabies welled up within us. Memories of the deepest attachments we felt in childhood flooded over us. With our babe in arms, we exulted in the miracle of newborn life, feeling an intense desire to do all in our power to surround him with love.

Jesus, Tender Shepherd, hear us. Bless thy little lamb tonight. In the darkness be thou near us. Keep us safe 'til morning light. Amen.

(*AT*, pp. 34, 75)

FIRST CHILD

If I had written the greatest book, composed the greatest symphony, painted the most beautiful painting or carved the most exquisite figure, I could not have felt more the exalted creator than I did when they placed my child in my arms. To think that this thing of beauty, sighing gently in my arms, reaching her little mouth for my breast, clutching at me with her tiny beautiful hands, had come from my flesh, was my child! Such a great feeling of happiness and joy filled me that I was hungry for Someone to thank, to love, even to worship, for so great a good that had been bestowed upon me. That tiny child was not enough to contain my love, nor could the father, though my heart was warm with love for both. . . . No human creature could receive or contain so vast a flood of love and joy. . . . With this came the need to worship, to adore.

> —*Dorothy Day, reflecting on her conversion,
> from* **Therese: A Life of Therese of Lisieux
> *and* The Long Loneliness: An Autobiography**

· · · · · · · · · · · · · · · · ·

Turning Our Hearts Toward Children

· · · · · · · · · · · · · · · · ·

With the spirit and power of Elijah he will go before him, to turn the hearts of parents to their children, and the disobedient to the wisdom of the righteous, to make ready a people prepared for the Lord.

—Luke 1:17

Birthing a child abruptly ushers us into a new world of awareness. Unfortunately, despite all that is said and written about parenthood, every new parent starts from scratch. We all have to learn on the job. It takes weeks, months, even years to become parents in our thoughts, feelings, and abilities. The rhythms and priorities of our lives change in the most profound and the most trivial ways. Simple daily routines become elaborate productions.

Tension between self-preservation and parental feelings arises. At times, as new parents, we are overwhelmed by the wonder of tiny fingers and toes and a soft cheek against ours. Euphoria stirred by love for this small creature can make us almost giddy. But other times we feel undone by the baby's demands, suddenly out of control of our lives, and immobilized by fatigue.

While passionately in love with this little person, we may experience him or her like an interruption to other important things we wanted to do. Yet at the same time, the baby's presence, in a mysterious way, brings sudden clarity about what *is* truly important.

At times we may feel our child's needs prevent us from following Christ. Other times it seems we're approaching a fuller understanding of God's work in our lives. In fact, there is a conversion in store for us when we allow God to turn our hearts toward the needs and joys of a little child.

You are changing us, Lord. Our hearts are expanding to include a child. And not only our hearts, but our schedules and priorities are radically shifting. Through all the change, we want you to remain central, the fixed point around which all else finds its place. Amen.

(*AT*, pp. 75–76, 80)

PERPETUAL PRAYER

But then the baby came home, and then you and others like you made a terrible, terribly lovely choice. You reached into your soul and withdrew that precious thing and lifted it up before your breast and began to walk. Deliberate and utterly beautiful, you strode to an altar of love for this child and placed there the talent, the dream, some core part of your particular *self*—and in order to mother another, you released it. There came for you a moment of conscious, sacred sacrifice. In that moment the self of yourself became a smoke, and the smoke went up to heaven as perpetual prayer for the sake of your children.

Children do not exist to please us. They are not *for* us at all. Rather, we exist for them—to protect them now and to prepare them for the future.

Who is given unto whom? Are children a gift to their elders? No—not till children are grown and their elders are older indeed. Then they are the gift of the fourth commandment, honoring hoary heads which have begun to feel past honor. But until then, it is we who are given, by God's parental mercy, to the children! And it is we who must give to the children—by lovely laughter, by laughter utterly free, and by the sheer joy from which such laughter springs—the lasting memory: *You are, you are, you are, my child, a marvelous work of God!*

> —*Walter Wangerin Jr.*, **Little Lamb, Who Made Thee?**[2]

· · · · · · · · · · · · · · · · ·

Why Would Anyone Dare?

· · · · · · · · · · · · · · · · ·

Peace I leave with you; my peace I give to you. I do not give to you as the world gives. Do not let your hearts be troubled, and do not let them be afraid.

—*John 14:27*

With a helpless infant in our care, our outlook on the world begins to undergo a revolutionary change. No longer are we simply responsible to watch out for ourselves amid all the precarious events of a normal day in this often dangerous world. Now we are thrusting a tiny, vulnerable person whom we cherish into the terrors and risks that arise on every hand. Innocence of babes in the language of poets denotes pure joy. But in the real world, the innocents are too often doomed to suffer its worst tragedies.

On bright spring days, with birds in song and trees bursting into blossom, we can almost believe that all is right with the world and our baby will grow to be brave, compassionate, and unscarred by mishap.

But then the news shatters our denial, and not only the news but the ugliness and pain in our own neighborhood. With a baby in arms, it's tough to muster up the courage to match the terror. With a baby in arms, how do we cope with the agony that is our world and will be his or her world?

Can we push back the madness and create an enclave of security for our children without becoming calloused toward other people in need? Can we enable our children to feel safe in God's love without unduly sheltering them? Can we teach hope to our children while grasping for hope ourselves?

As difficult as it is sometimes, for our children's sake, we must. They draw their bedrock security from our confidence that everything is fundamentally all right. And we draw our confidence from the One who has promised that everything will be all right.

We're worried and afraid, Father, we can't deny it. As hard as we try to protect our little one, much will happen that we wouldn't have chosen. May you, even in these early days, cause all that happens to work for good in the life of our beloved child, now and always. Amen.

(*AT*, pp. 24–25)

IT'S ALL RIGHT

Then she turns toward me, reaches for me. "I'm scared. I'm scared."

I put my arms around her and hold her. I hold her as I held my children when they were small and afraid in the night; as, this summer, I hold my grandchildren. I hold her as she, once upon a time and long ago, held me. And I say the same words, the classic, maternal, instinctive words of reassurance. "Don't be afraid. I'm here. It's all right."

"Something's wrong. I'm scared. I'm scared."

I cradle her and repeat, "It's all right."

What's all right? What am I promising her? I'm scared too. I don't know what will happen when Hugh goes to the neurologist. I don't know what's going to happen to my mother this summer. I don't know what the message may be the next time the phone rings. What's all right? How can I say it?

But I do. I hold her close, and kiss her, and murmur, "It's all right, Mother. It's all right."

I mean these words. I do not understand them, but I mean them.

> —*Madeleine L'Engle*, **The Summer of the Great-Grandmother**

. . . .

Rock-A-My-Soul

. . . .

O LORD, my heart is not lifted up, my eyes are not raised too high; I do not occupy myself with things too great and too marvelous for me.

But I have calmed and quieted my soul, like a weaned child with its mother; my soul within me is like a weaned child.

—*Psalm 131:1-2*

There are few more satisfying moments than when a baby gives up the struggle, totally relaxes in one's arms, and drifts into peaceful oblivion. The baby who only a few moments before had been flailing, frantically crying out, now blissfully nestles into rest. After filling her aching stomach and feeling kind arms around her, she relaxes and with absolute trust sinks against her father's broad chest with total abandon.

And having calmed his child, the father also can rest deeply. Trust and nurture flow both ways. As the little one receives what she needs, she gives back to her father and mother the profound satisfaction that comes from mutual fulfillment. The nurturer's spirit is nurtured even as he cares for another.

Many of the joys of parenting are indescribable and unanticipated, involving a quality of love that surprises us with its intensity. Our desire to care adequately for our child is so great that when we succeed, the relief and joy that envelop us carry us heavenward if we allow it, into the arms of our Maker. There we rest with abandon, knowing that the one who cares for us is also an ever watchful, ever loving Parent.

Lord, bring us into that place of quiet rest, near to your heart. May the contentment we experience in your embrace calm our spirits so we can rock our baby into rest day after endless day. Amen.

THERE IS A PLACE OF QUIET REST

There is a place of quiet rest,
  near to the heart of God,
a place where sin cannot molest,
  near to the heart of God.

Refrain:
O Jesus, bless'd Redeemer,
  sent from the heart of God,
hold us, who wait before thee,
  near to the heart of God.

There is a place of comfort sweet,
  near to the heart of God,
a place where we our Savior meet,
  near to the heart of God.

There is a place of full release,
  near to the heart of God,
a place where all is joy and peace,
  near to the heart of God.

—Cleland B. McAfee in **Hymnal,
A Worship Book**

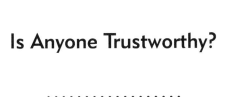

Is Anyone Trustworthy?

Can a woman forget her nursing child, or show no compassion for the child of her womb? Even these may forget, yet I will not forget you.

—Isaiah 49:15

No advance warnings about a baby's impact could have prepared us for the tricks our psyche would play on us. Dreams haunted Sara, suggesting that she might go off to town and forget her baby alone at home. Gerald worried in new ways about traffic hazards and financial insecurities. Anxiety about whether or not we knew how to care for our baby wasn't helped by insensitive suggestions from those who presumably knew all about baby care.

There is no end to the specialties we new parents are expected to master. We scramble, scrub, and stand watch—anything to keep ahead of the towering wave of guilt that threatens to come crashing down if someone insinuates that we've been negligent.

Would a momentary lapse into our carefree, pre-parental behavior actually be possible? Could we who have been accountable only for our own comings and goings suddenly be adequately responsible for a round-the-clock vigil over a helpless baby? Our baby's birth requires nothing less than an altered state of consciousness, an upheaval in our psychological orientation.

As parents we are entrusted with a sacred and immensely heavy responsibility to care for our child. We are expected to be and want to be *totally* trustworthy. But we know we won't be. We will fail. We are human.

God is contrasted with a nursing mother who could *perhaps* forget her offspring, though it seems highly unlikely. But, God suggests, *I* will not forget you. It is reassuring to know God is completely trustworthy. No matter how badly we mess up, "The LORD is merciful and gracious, slow to anger and abounding in steadfast love" (Psalm 103:8).

Without your mercy, gracious God, we would be lost because this task is huge. Free us to do our best and then leave the rest to you. And forgive us when we fail. Amen.

(*AT*, pp. 96–97)

QUIET MINISTRY

It is good to experience the quiet ministry of the living spirit of the living God. Again and again there are the little healings of silent breaches which sustain us in our contacts with the world and with one another. We are stunned by the little word, the unexpected silence, the smile off key; without quite knowing why, the balance is recovered and the rhythm of the hurt is stopped in its place. There is the sense of estrangement which over-takes the happiest human relations and the experience of recovery that makes the heart sing its old song with a new lilt. There are days when everything seems difficult, when the ordinary tasks become major undertakings, when one is sensitive and every moment is threatened by an explosion that does not quite come to pass; then without apparent cause, the whole picture changes and the spirit can breathe again with ease, the spring in the step comes back again. It is good to experience the quiet ministry of the living spirit of the living God.

—*Howard Thurman*, **The Inward Journey**[3]

. . . .

Parents Are Human Too

. . . .

My grace is sufficient for you, for power is made perfect in weakness.

—2 Corinthians 12:9

By becoming parents all of us entered a new realm of uncertainty. We opened ourselves to certain pain and likely failure. Yet in doing so we also opened ourselves to the possibility of experiencing a new dimension of God's grace.

All will likely not turn out as we hope for our children. Children are infinitely complex, perpetually unpredictable. We can't guarantee that even our best efforts will produce anything resembling what we hope they will become. We do well to acknowledge our capacity to err rather than to live nervously under the illusion that there is a foolproof formula for producing perfect progeny. There isn't. Christ's strength is made perfect in our weakness. Christ can redeem even when "perfect" techniques fail.

Parents are like artists. We may recognize our own distinctive brush strokes of color on the canvas, but so many subtle tones will be added by others that the composite of color and line may sometimes be alarming, sometimes mysterious, sometimes beautiful.

The final harmonizing of the many different brush strokes belongs to a Master Artist. If and when our children grow to resemble even remotely what we hoped and prayed they would become, their beauty will be a miracle of grace—the gift of the Master Artist. "In a very real sense," Madeleine L'Engle writes about artists in *Walking on Water*, "not one of us is qualified, but it seems that God continually chooses the most unqualified to do his work, to bear his glory. If we are qualified, we tend to think that we have done the job ourselves. If we are forced to accept our evident lack of qualification, then there's no danger that we will confuse God's work with our own, or God's glory with our own."

This unfinished masterpiece, Creator God, is from your studio. We are thrilled with the opportunity to assist in shaping its form and beauty, but we are also relieved that ultimately the finished work is yours to accomplish. Work beside us, God, so our strokes are in harmony with yours. Amen.

(*TM*, June 14, 1994)

PATIENCE

Everything is gestation and then bringing forth. To let each impression and each germ of a feeling come to completion wholly in itself, in the dark, in the inexpressible, the unconscious, beyond the reach of one's own intelligence, and await with deep humility and patience the birth-hour of a new clarity: that alone is living the artist's life: in understanding as in creating.

There is here no measuring with time, no year matters, and ten years are nothing. Being an artist means, not reckoning and counting, but ripening like the tree which does not force its sap and stands confident in the storms of spring without the fear that after them may come no summer. It does come. But it comes only to the patient, who are there as though eternity lay before them, so unconcernedly still and wide, I learn it daily, learn it with pain to which I am grateful: patience is everything!

—Rainer Maria Rilke, **Letters to a Young Poet**

. . . .

We Love Because We Are Loved

. . . .

I have made your name known to them, and I will make it known, so that the love with which you have loved me may be in them, and I in them.

—John 17:26

A child's love is not instinctive, not even a heritable trait, writes Selma Fraiberg in *Every Child's Birthright*. A child loves because he is loved. The exuberance, the smiles, the excited kicking of a baby are not mere abilities in his innate repertoire, but evidence that the baby's human partners have made him glad to be alive.

The more we understand that the shape of a lifetime is set by our day-to-day, moment-by-moment reassurance of goodness, the more diligently we will embrace parenting as a God-ordained vocation. The choice is ours, either to give ourselves wholeheartedly to this most foundational job, or increasingly to resent its endless demands. The daily commitment to small acts of kindness and courtesy makes all the difference between a family who slowly disintegrates and one who comes to know the joy of companionship.

Parenting is a sacred ministry of reproducing love. When we know we are beloved by God we love in turn, even sacrificially, so that love will be reborn generation after generation. We too love because we are first loved by another.

Awaken love in our hearts, Lord God, and keep it strong and vibrant. Somehow, when we're in love with you, our love for each other increases and we're able to care for our child even when the demands seem endless. We hope too that our child will learn to love you because love has flourished in our home. Amen.

(*AT*, p. 101)

OUT OF SOLITUDE

In solitude we can slowly unmask the illusion of our possessiveness and discover in the center of our own self that we are not what we can conquer, but what is given to us. In solitude we can listen to the voice of him who spoke to us before we could speak a word, who healed us before we could make any gesture to help, who set us free long before we could free others, and who loved us long before we could give love to anyone. It is in this solitude that we discover that being is more important than having, and that we are worth more than the result of our efforts. In solitude we discover that our life is not a possession to be defended, but a gift to be shared. It's there we recognize that the healing words we speak are not just our own, but are given to us; that the love we can express is part of a greater love, and that the new life we bring forth is not a property to cling to, but a gift to be received.

—*Henri J. Nouwen*, Out of Solitude

. . . .

Godly Parents

. . . .

Honor your father and your mother, so that your days
may be long in the land that the LORD is giving you.

—*Exodus 20:12*

. . . .

Like a Living Sacrifice

. . . .

I appeal to you therefore, brothers and sisters, by the mercies of God, to present your bodies as a living sacrifice, holy and acceptable to God, which is your spiritual worship.

—Romans 12:1

The idea of a living sacrifice never seemed more real to Sara than during those many nights she sat up nursing a distraught, colicky baby. Usually just getting to the end of a day seemed a formidable feat, and then the night of piercing yells for Mother's milk and Daddy's arms stretched ahead.

For new parents, gone are uninterrupted nights of blissful sleep. Gone are leisurely, long hours of undisturbed husband-wife companionship. Our clocks are now set to another's rhythm. Our patterns must now adjust to another's demands.

Often along with the major shift in time investment come ambivalent feelings and soul searching about who I am, who my spouse is now that we're so preoccupied with childcare. Will we be trapped forever? Will we ever feel free again to come and go at will? Will we lose out on the progress we had been making in our jobs? Nagging questions of self doubt quickly sap energy.

It was the awakening love for our child that saved us. A miracle broke on us in a momentary flash of acceptance about the sacrifices we were being called on to make—a miracle of a relationship with a child that we wouldn't trade for the world.

We decided to savor the *now*, lest in striving for some elusive future achievement we overlook the beauty of the moments we have right now.

All we have, after all, are little moments crammed with a multitude of things for which to be grateful. And it is in living them faithfully that our sacrifice becomes worship and prepares us for whatever else God may ask of us.

Dear Lord, may the offering of our time and energy for another make us newly aware of your sacrifice for us. You gave your life so that we could have life. Teach us to do the same, whatever it costs. Amen.

(*AT*, pp. 83–84)

MAGIC

I suppose to some extent all children have a touch of magic about them—like some mysterious living lens they seem to have the capacity to focus the light into the darkest and gloomiest of places. . . . Perhaps it's the very newness of the young, or perhaps it's just because the shine hasn't worn off, but they can and do, if you give them half a chance, make a dent in the toughest armour of life. If you're very lucky they can dissolve away all those protective barricades so carefully erected over years of living.

—*Fynn*, Mister God, This is Anna

. . . .

KEY MOMENTS

Taking your children to school and kissing your wife good-bye. Eating lunch with a friend. Trying to do a decent day's work. Hearing the rain patter against the window. There is no event so commonplace but that God is present within it, always hiddenly, always leaving you room to recognize him, but all the more fascinatingly because of that, all the more compellingly and hauntingly. . . . In the boredom and pain of it no less than in the excitement and gladness: touch, taste, smell your way to the holy and hidden heart of it because in the last analysis all moments are key moments, and life itself is grace.

—*Frederick Buechner*, Now and Then

A New Spiritual Discipline

Whoever becomes humble like this child is the greatest in the kingdom of heaven. Whoever welcomes one such child in my name welcomes me.

—Matthew 18:4-5

One hears a lot of talk in some circles about spiritual disciplines like prayer, fasting, meditation, and simplicity. Another discipline could be added to the list—parenting. If we care for our children as Jesus would, it becomes a profound, life-changing discipline of the spirit. There is perhaps no more significant sign that one is a disciple of Jesus Christ than welcoming children with a tender, caring heart.

Jesus says, "Whoever welcomes a little child like this in my name welcomes me." He implies that whoever refuses to welcome a child rejects Jesus and the One who sent him.

Babies don't ask to be born. Nor do they promise to fit into our lifestyle. They simply *are*. In their weakness, they compel us toward costly choices that go against all we've been programmed to expect for ourselves.

To embrace parenting as a spiritual discipline is to put children first for a season. It doesn't mean doting on them as the ultimate meaning of our existence. Nor does it mean turning them into showcase models of our excellent parenting. We put them first because they come to us as Christ did, weak and vulnerable. Christ comes to us in and through them.

We firmly believe that when we are ministering to children we are *with* Jesus in a unique way. In truth, whoever welcomes a little child, welcomes Jesus himself.

Jesus, as we welcome our small, weak one, we also welcome you. May we grow in grace and knowledge of you as we serve the little one you've entrusted to our care. Amen.

(*CH*, pp. 11–13)

SACRAMENT OF CARING

Living the sacrament of the care for others draws a person close to the greatest of all truths. It does this better than anything else can, but it does this in ways that are seldom obvious. It is for this reason that it is a spiritual discipline. Those who first sought the desert and found themselves alone, with little food, little water, and nothing to stand between themselves and God, did not feel immediate inspiration. All they found at first was loneliness, hunger, thirst, and temptations. It was only later, after living their life with prayer and carefully listening to the words spoken within the heart, that they learned the truth hidden within the struggle they had chosen. The same is true here. Only after living the sacrament of care day after day and working as much as possible to find within it the aspect of prayer does this life begin to reveal itself as one joined to the most powerful truth there is.

It is then that the sacrament of caring reveals its special connection with God. To live this life is to participate in the mystery of the divine and to become a partner in that ongoing act of creation, the forming of the love from which all else is formed. . . . Only love and what love forms endure.

—*Ernest Boyer Jr.*, Finding God at Home

. . . .

The Fruit of the Spirit

. . . .

By contrast, the fruit of the Spirit is love, joy, peace, patience, kindness, generosity, faithfulness, gentleness, and self-control. There is no law against such things.

—Galatians 5:22-23

On becoming parents we have found that those who fail in their responsibilities as parents have a new claim on our sympathy. It is said that, "To be a father rather than a son is to learn the inevitability of failure."

Emotions we thought we possessed only in manageable quantities now rear their heads with vigor. We feel anger, impatience, exasperation, selfishness. A baby arrives clothed in pristine freshness, a bundle of perfection. She should rightfully be placed in the hands of perfect, saintly parents. Children deserve the very best! These innocent, trusting, impressionable cherubs should be given the optimum conditions for flowering into their full potential. Anything less feels like a travesty of justice. But these brand-new beauties get us! Fallible, fumbling, half-baked adults. We sincerely want to do our best, but often find that's a lot harder than we thought.

Parenting is likely the most difficult job we will ever undertake. The patience, tolerance, wisdom, and physical and emotional energy required of a parent in a single day are phenomenal. We continually have the feeling that we should have more to give, even while showing strengths we didn't know we had.

Our daily prayer must be to grow in the fruits of the Spirit so our exasperation and complaining give way to love, joy, peace, patience, kindness, generosity, faithfulness, gentleness, and self-control. With a commitment to grow in these life-giving qualities, the Spirit's goodness among us will supersede our own failures.

Without your Spirit bearing fruit in our lives, Lord, we would become a bundle of tension, impatience, and anger. Bear fruit in us so we can model what we want our child to become—a loving, generous, and self-controlled adult. Amen.

(*AT*, pp. 108–109, 117)

TO PRAY

People who pray, really pray, don't talk about it much. After
you have looked into the matter carefully, you may be able
to puzzle out who is really praying. In general, though,
prayer is something of an underground. Is it because people
who pray are too possessive about their experiences to
share them? On the contrary, people who pray usually share
their experiences generously. But on the whole they don't
advertise their prayer lives. Perhaps the energy that might
be used in talk goes to prayer instead.

To find a person who prays, you have to look for clues:
charitableness, good temper, patience, a fair ability to handle stress, resonance, openness to others. What happens
to people who pray is that their inward life gradually takes
over from their outward life. That is not to say that they are
any less active. They may be competent lawyers, doctors,
businessmen. But their hearts lie in the inner life and they
are moved by that.

> —*Emilie Griffin*, **Clinging: The Experience of
> Prayer**

. . . .

Mom and Dad Were Human Too

. . . .

"Honor your father and mother"—this is the first commandment with a promise: "so that it may be well with you and you may live long on the earth."

—Ephesians 6:2-3

After becoming parents we gained new awareness that *our* parents were persons first—men and women, who among other accomplishments, raised children. We felt reconnected with the humanity we share with our parents because we had become what they are. It was as if we were seeing them as complex, developing, searching persons in their own right rather than merely as Mom and Dad.

It used to seem as if perhaps parents encouraged their children toward birthing the next generation to perpetuate the family line or because they were eager to become doting grandparents. But after becoming parents ourselves, it occurred to us that perhaps parents long for their children to become parents so that they can receive empathy from their often unappreciative offspring. Those who have gone before seem to sense some historic justice when we youngsters give up our irresponsible childishness and begin to devote ourselves to caring for another's needs.

Is it too much to hope that when children have grown beyond their arrogant youth and sense their own limitations as new parents, they may extend forgiveness and honor toward their own parents?

The link between how we were parented and how we will parent is inescapable. Becoming parents nudges us to examine patterns in our own family that for good or ill will affect how we parent. The better we understand our own parents, the sooner we can forgive them and honor them for the good that was there. Such awareness frees us to confess our own failures and call on God and our community to help us in our parenting.

Lord, we want to be a faithful link in the generations, extending honor to our own parents for the way they have served us, even though it was imperfect. We want to freely acknowledge our own failures and live in the grace of your forgiveness every day. Amen.

(*AT*, p. 117)

MERCY ON ME

Have mercy on me, O God,
   according to your steadfast love;
   according to your abundant mercy
   blot out my transgressions.
Wash me thoroughly from my iniquity,
   and cleanse me from my sin.
For I know my transgressions, and my sin is ever before me.
Against you, you alone, have I sinned,
   and done what is evil in your sight,
   so that you are justified in your sentence
   and blameless when you pass judgment.
Purge me with hyssop, and I shall be clean;
   wash me, and I shall be whiter than snow.
Let me hear joy and gladness;
   let the bones that you have crushed rejoice.
Hide your face from my sins, and blot out all my iniquities.
Create in me a clean heart, O God,
   and put a new and right spirit within me.
Do not cast me away from your presence,
   and do not take your holy spirit from me.
Restore to me the joy of your salvation,
   and sustain in me a willing spirit.

—Psalm 51:1-4, 7-12

· · · · · · · · · · · · · · · · ·

Slow Down and Simplify

· · · · · · · · · · · · · · · · ·

Therefore I tell you, do not worry about your life, what you will eat or what you will drink, or about your body, what you will wear. Is not life more than food, and the body more than clothing? . . . Indeed your heavenly Father knows that you need all these things. But strive first for the kingdom of God and his righteousness, and all these things will be given to you as well.

—Matthew 6:25, 32-33

When we become parents it is crucial that we slow down and simplify our lives. We usually arrange time for what we consider truly important—and when our child is small, moving along at her pace *is* truly important. It's often said that children get in the way. If so, perhaps we should ask where we're going. By going a few paces in our child's direction we'll likely arrive where we should.

We rush and shove our little ones along—hurrying them here and there. We're in grave danger of imposing our own agenda on them inappropriately or neglecting them because of our own priorities. When we're free to sit with our child, hold her, read to her, and dangle our toes in the pond with her, then our relationship will blossom.

Many of us can eat and live more simply to limit our income needs and make room for more time with our child. There are things money can't buy—our precious child and the simple pleasure of growing little with her and entering into *life*.

We cope better at this stage by accepting less demanding outside involvements and coming down "where we ought to be . . . in the place just right," with our child. Unless we learn to slow down and cherish time with our children, we will have had the experience, as T. S. Eliot warned, but missed the meaning.

Free us to slow down, Lord, and simplify our lives. Free us from the stress of needing to achieve and the anxiety about providing adequately. Bring us to a deeper level of trust in you to provide. Amen.

(*AT*, pp. 120–121, 189)

SIMPLE GIFTS

'Tis a gift to be simple,
'Tis a gift to be free;
'Tis a gift to come down
   where we ought to be.
And when we find ourselves in the place
   just right,
'Twill be in the valley
   of love and delight.

When true simplicity is gained,
To bow and to bend
   We will not be ashamed.
To turn, turn
   will be our delight,
'Til by turning, turning
   we come round right.

—*Shaker song*, **Simple Gifts**

. . . .

A Sacred Interlude

. . . .

Jesus said to her, "Everyone who drinks of this water will be thirsty again, but those who drink of the water that I will give them will never be thirsty. The water that I will give will become in them a spring of water gushing up to eternal life."

—John 4:13-15

There should be a sacred interlude for every parent within the pattern of a day when each can retire into his or her own space and be replenished from the inner spring. Every parent needs time alone to maintain that connection with the source of refreshment. Unless we take time out to nourish our own spirits, we will find ourselves parched and unable to be what we want to be for our children.

The truth is, we need nurture if we are going to nurture. We are much more able to give love after just fifteen minutes of quiet in the presence of the One who sustains us.

One of the most important things a young parent must assert is that in the midst of all the giving there are some things one cannot afford to give up. Time alone is one of those things. We need to know ourselves as beloved of God and bask in that love. We also need to know ourselves as friends, partners, creative persons distinct from our responsibilities as parents. Time alone or away, even though brief gives us perspective and renews our spirits.

Persons who respect their own need for quiet and space will teach children to respect that need. Our children will learn by example to appreciate creative silence and to find their own bubbling inner springs.

Still small voice, teach us to so order our days that we will find space to listen to you, and be renewed. Be a spring of water for us that refreshes and brightens our spirits. Reassure us every day that we are beloved no matter what. Amen.

(*AT*, pp. 122–123)

PERFECT PLACE

My special place is a small brook in a green glade, a circle of quiet from which there is no visible sign of human beings. There's a natural stone bridge over the brook, and I sit there, dangling my legs and looking through the foliage at the sky reflected in the water, and things slowly come back into perspective. If the insects are biting me—and they usually are; no place is quite perfect—I use the pliable branch of a shadblow tree as a fan. The brook wanders through a tunnel of foliage, and the birds sing more sweetly there than anywhere else; or perhaps it is just that when I am at the brook I have time to be aware of them, and I move slowly into a kind of peace that is marvelous, "annihilating all that's made to a green thought in a green shade." If I sit for awhile, then my impatience, crossness, frustration, are indeed annihilated, and my sense of humor returns.

—Madeleine L'Engle, A Circle of Quiet

Cycles of Eternity

Lord, you have been our dwelling place in all generations. Before the mountains were brought forth, or ever you had formed the earth and the world, from everlasting to everlasting you are God.

—Psalm 90:1-2

When we become parents we understand in a new way the "cycles of eternity," as Ernest Boyer Jr. calls them. For first time parents, our tiny newborn seems a miracle as fresh as if a birth had never occurred before in human history. Our eyes and hearts are opened to a world of awareness we had only dimly known secondhand.

Then our fresh born beauty grows into a child, an adult, leaves home, marries, and gives birth to yet another new beginning. A springtime has come again before anyone realized the old one had passed. The parents, now grandparents, "rediscover the meaning of their own spring," writes Boyer. They find it is not diminished because it has passed, but enriched because it has been repeated.

This is the great gift of the spirituality of the family and the covenant of parenthood in particular, says Boyer: "direct participation in the cycles of eternity and the opportunity to see within the process of individual love the working of a greater Love."

Sometimes in the dark as we stand beside the bed of our sleeping child, our hearts throb with remorse. Our exasperation and impatience of the day past seem tawdry beside our beautiful, trusting cherub. Now asleep, he is the picture of peace. Would that as his many demands ricochet through our day, we could embrace him as a gift to teach us, share life with us, remind us of our own beginnings and our approaching end.

Alpha and Omega, the way ahead is long. There will be many beginnings and endings as we cycle through the years. We want you to be with us at the beginnings and at the endings. We want you to be our dwelling place, our one constant home amid all changes. Amen.

(*AT*, pp. 124–125)

SIMPLIFICATION

But there is a deeper, an internal simplification of the whole of one's personality, stilled, tranquil, in childlike trust listening ever to Eternity's whisper, walking with a smile into the dark.

This amazing simplification comes when we "center down," when life is lived with singleness of eye, from a holy Center where the breath and stillness of Eternity are heavy upon us and we are wholly yielded to Him. Some of you know this holy, recreating Center of eternal peace and joy and live in it day and night. Some of you may see it over the margin and wistfully long to slip into that amazing Center where the soul is at home with God. Be very faithful to that wistful longing.

—Thomas R. Kelly, **A Testament of Devotion**

. . . .

It's a Lot More Fun to Share

. . . .

As a father has compassion for his children, so the LORD has compassion for those who fear him.

—Psalm 103:13

Her children rise up and call her happy; her husband too, and he praises her: "Many women have done excellently, but you surpass them all."

—Proverbs 31:28

New parents are suddenly confronted with the question of who does what when for the baby. Though both parents may be committed to the attentive presence of mother and father, how that works out practically must be negotiated day by day.

Good quality of childcare is a strong argument for shared parenting. Everyone benefits as mother and father share the load, especially the child. Many fathers have deserted their children, leaving them essentially fatherless. And without adequate support, motherhood is a quick road to losing control and hurting oneself and one's children.

A structure of shared household responsibilities frees each spouse to enjoy parenting rather than being undone by it. There is no perfect way to share. Each couple must find the arrangement that serves them best. The mutual relationship of love and respect that we want in our homes is one in which compromises are made on the basis of what is fair for each and best for our relationship and for the child.

Most parenting skills don't come naturally for father or mother. Learning them becomes part of a process that forms us more fully into the image of our Maker. Both husband and wife are called to serve God, sharing the good news as they are gifted. Each is responsible to facilitate the other's best ability to minister, both at home and abroad. This is the biblical vision of mutuality and what a glorious vision it is.

Holy One, as we adjust to this new responsibility help us to be sensitive to each other. Help us to listen carefully for the deep longings and needs of our partner. We want to find ways to better enable each other to parent happily and creatively. Amen.

(*AT*, pp. 128–135)

WILL YOU LET ME BE YOUR SERVANT

Will you let me be your servant,
 let me be as Christ to you?
Pray that I may have the grace
 to let you be my servant too.

We are pilgrims on a journey,
 we are trav'lers on the road.
We are here to help each other
 walk the mile and bear the load.

I will hold the Christ-light for you
 in the nighttime of your fear.
I will hold my hand out to you,
 speak the peace you long to hear.

I will weep when you are weeping,
 when you laugh I'll laugh with you.
I will share your joy and sorrow
 till we've seen this journey through.

When we sing to God in heaven,
 we shall find such harmony,
born of all we've known together
 of Christ's love and agony.

—*Richard Gillard, in* **Hymnal, A Worship Book**[4]

. . . .

Parenthood Solidarity

. . . .

People were bringing little children to him in order that he might touch them; and the disciples spoke sternly to them. But when Jesus saw this, he was indignant and said to them, "Let the little children come to me; do not stop them; for it is to such as these that the kingdom of God belongs."

—Mark 10:13-14

Becoming parents sensitized us to the suffering of parents and their little ones everywhere. Parenthood humanized us, making us much more aware of basic human need. We understood as never before that when a father or mother is unable to provide food and medical care for their little ones, it is the cruelest of tragedies!

With the Hebrew prophet Hosea we hear an enraged God rebuking Israel, "When I fed them, they were satisfied; they were satisfied, and their heart was proud; therefore they forgot me. So I will become like a lion to them, like a leopard. I will lurk beside the way. I will fall upon them like a bear robbed of her cubs" (Hosea 13:6-8a).

God identifies with the enraged mother bear whose cubs have been taken away. God pursues their captors with an anger beyond that of any parent whose little one has been robbed of food, healthcare, a chance to live, love, laugh. "Truly I tell you, just as you did not do it to one of the least of these, you did not do it to me" (Matthew 25:45). Those who care for the least of these are rewarded with eternal life, Jesus declared. Those who disregard or merely tolerate the least of these gain eternal punishment.

As we held our helpless infant, we felt moved to nurture not only his life, but the life of every child. Our children are not given us so we can dote only on them. Our task is bigger than preserving our own family. Because of and with our children, we are compelled to reach out to other children and their parents. "Let the children come to me."

Jesus, Lover of children, may the arrival of our child sensitize our hearts to other children. May we, along with our child, bring other children to you for blessing. Amen.

(*AT*, pp. 163–164, 179–180)

SPRING?

When some of us look at children, especially when they are happy, we feel what the Jesuit poet Gerard Manley Hopkins was expressing in a poem called "Spring" when he asked: "What is all this juice and all this joy?" For us, children are the springtime, the creative burgeoning of human life. They are not only *in* that springtime; they *are* that springtime. . . . They seem to breathe their own excess of vitality into the things they touch or try to touch. Their surprise (and they are themselves surprises) sometimes makes us older ones want to draw close to them, the way a freezing traveler wants to stop his purposeful voyage in order to draw close to a warm and lambent fire.

And when they are tortured, when they are deliberately broken and killed, it is spring that is being attacked. It is as if the living center of human life were being dirtied and then smashed. . . . There is an unbridgeable difference between those who can torture and destroy children and those who can only save them.

—Philip Hallie, **Lest Innocent Blood Be Shed**

. . . .

Out of the Mouths of Babes

. . . .

But when the chief priests and the scribes saw the amazing things that he did, and heard the children crying out in the temple, "Hosanna to the Son of David," they became angry and said to him, "Do you hear what these are saying?" Jesus said to them, "Yes; have you never read, 'Out of the mouths of infants and nursing babies you have prepared praise for yourself?'"

—*Matthew 21:14-16*

Our first son used to say, "When you get little like I am . . ." His mother laughed and explained he had it backwards. On further reflection, however, perhaps he was closer to the truth than she. Somehow it seems that unless we adults "get little" we can never hope to enter into kingdom life with abandon and joy like Jesus intends.

What is so special about little people? Are children really so far ahead of us in grasping the essence of the kingdom, as Jesus seems to imply? Is their praise purer than ours?

In God's scheme, growing small, becoming a child, and befriending children have everything to do with acquiring wisdom. Little children shatter our facades. With affection and charm they snuggle against our aching lonely hearts. They unmask our adult reserve and release the pent up part of us that longs for birth, for play, for praise. Children restore for us a sense of wonder. We rediscover the world through their fresh, sensuous perspectives—and we worship. Staying close to children means staying close to new life.

Children make us laugh with elation for being human, despite dust-to-dust and all the rest. Children put the Ah! back into the mixture of "mess and marvel which makes the mystery of our mortal life."

A well-known elderly psychologist said, "If there's any part of my life I'd give anything to do over, it would be to experience, on a day-to-day basis, the pleasure of my children. I guess I thought they would wait to grow up until I'd gotten everything done."

Lord, as our child awakens to the world, may his or her joy and wonder awaken us to praise you. Open our eyes to see you through the eyes of our child. Amen.

(*AT*, pp. 181–183, 186–189)

PIED BEAUTY

Glory be to God for dappled things—
   For skies of couple-colour as a brinded cow;
     For rose-moles in all stipple upon trout that swim;
Fresh-firecoal chestnut-falls; finches' wings;
   Landscape plotted and pieced—fold, fallow, and plough;
     And all trades, their gear and tackle and trim.

All things counter, original, spare, strange;
   Whatever is fickle, freckled (who knows how?)
     With swift, slow; sweet, sour; adazzle, dim;
He fathers-forth whose beauty is past change:
   Praise him.

                 —*Gerard Manley Hopkins*, Poems and Prose

. . . .

A Parenting God

. . . .

He will turn the hearts of parents to their children
and the hearts of children to their parents.

—Malachi 4:6

. . . .

Birth—A Hopeful Sign of the Times

. . . .

For the creation waits with eager longing for the revealing of the children of God; . . . We know that the whole creation has been groaning in labor pains until now; and not only the creation, but we ourselves, who have the first fruits of the Spirit, groan inwardly while we wait for adoption, the redemption of our bodies.

—Romans 8:19, 22, 23

To bear a child into a world threatened with ecological disaster, overpopulation, widespread violence—this is more than an act of wishful hope. It is an act of defiance, a bold step of faith in which we stake our lives and that of our child on God's future.

Birth is ever a renewal of hope—the stuff of the kingdom not founded in this world. The groans of travail that Paul heard ringing through creation are the birth pangs of a new age, the hope of a future yet unseen.

Those of us birthing children today are not naive about the odds. Jim Wallis, editor of *Sojourners*, suggests that, "It is precisely because the times are so bad that we need to plant, build and create new life. . . . To give up is to succumb to despair and unbelief."

What is incredible is that godly men and women persevere. In our individual worlds we hold the forces of evil at bay. Each of us who refuses to give in to apathy and despair sparks around us a movement of hope.

Mary, a woman of faith, understood that hidden within her was hope for an aching world. Through her child, a world was turned upside down. Our babies are not messiahs. Yet with Mary we too are moved to magnify the one who has shown strength, scattered the proud, and exalted those of low degree. We rejoice in our children who endure as a sign of hope amidst despair. We trust they will cherish our earth, carry torches of light into the next generation, and endure as God's new gesture of good will toward all.

We dedicate our children to you, dear Savior. We trust you to fill our darlings with your joy, so no matter what happens they will know with whom their future lies. Amen.

(*AT*, pp. 201–202, 207)

MARY'S SONG OF PRAISE

And Mary said,
  "My soul magnifies the Lord,
    and my spirit rejoices in God my Savior,
  for he has looked with favor on the lowliness of his servant.
    Surely, from now on all generations will call me blessed;
  for the Mighty One has done great things for me,
    and holy is his name.
  His mercy is for those who fear him
    from generation to generation.
  He has shown strength with his arm;
    he has scattered the proud in the thoughts of their hearts.
  He has brought down the powerful from their thrones,
    and lifted up the lowly;
  he has filled the hungry with good things,
    and sent the rich away empty.
  He has helped his servant Israel,
    in remembrance of his mercy,
  according to the promise he made to our ancestors,
    to Abraham and to his descendants forever."

—Luke 1:46-55

· · · · · · · · · · · · · · · · ·

Nothing Can Separate Us

· · · · · · · · · · · · · · · · ·

No, in all these things we are more than conquerors through him who loved us. For I am convinced that neither death, nor life, nor angels, nor rulers, nor things present, nor things to come, nor powers, nor height, nor depth, nor anything else in all creation, will be able to separate us from the love of God in Christ Jesus our Lord.

—Romans 8:37-39

Our child snuggled securely in his mother's arms. "Are you taking care of me?" His eyes were filled with the question. "Yes, Mama and Daddy will take care of you, dear one. You are precious beyond reckoning and we *will* take care of you."

Little did he know how helpless we are to protect him from all harm. Yet we have found a faith, a hope by which to live. Whether in pain, in danger, in poverty, or in prosperity, we believe that nothing, absolutely nothing, can separate us from the love of God.

To be alive is to be vulnerable. To be born is to start traveling toward death. Yet childbirth is an affirmation of life, a rebuttal of death. Newness and goodness of life come from the Giver of good. Hope is a gift of the Spirit, a gift that, like laughter, can be contagious. We can live in hope and instill it in our children.

We can't be sure bad things will never come. But because of our bottom-line confidence we can say that no matter what happens, nothing can separate us from God's love. Not disease nor accident. Not personal failure nor indiscriminate terror. We can rock our children to sleep every night reassuring them of that foundational truth.

Lord God, it would be hard to deal with all of our fears and our child's fears if we didn't know that no matter what, your love can still reach and hold us. Thank you above all for that promise. All else depends on it. Amen.

(*AT*, pp. 210–211)

INTERRUPTIONS

A few years ago I met an old professor at the University of Notre Dame. Looking back on his long life of teaching, he said with a funny twinkle in his eyes: "I have always been complaining that my work was constantly interrupted, until I slowly discovered that my interruptions were my work."

That is the great conversion in our life: to recognize and believe that the many unexpected events are not just disturbing interruptions of our projects, but the way in which God molds our hearts and prepares us for his return. Our great temptations are boredom and bitterness. When our good plans are interrupted by poor weather, our well-organized careers by illness or bad luck, our peace of mind by inner turmoil, our hope for peace by a new war, our desire for a stable government by a constant changing of the guards, and our desire for immortality by real death, we are tempted to give in to a paralyzing boredom or to strike back in destructive bitterness. But when we believe that patience can make our expectations grow, then fate can be converted into a vocation, wounds into a call for deeper understanding, and sadness into a birthplace of joy.

—Henri J. Nouwen, Out of Solitude[5]

. . . .

Every, Every Minute

. . . .

You shall put these words of mine in your heart and soul
. . . bind them as a sign on your hand, and fix them as an
emblem on your forehead. Teach them to your children,
talking about them when you are at home and when you
are away, when you lie down and when you rise. Write them
on the doorposts of your house and on your gates, so that
your days and the days of your children may be multiplied in
the land . . .

—Deuteronomy 11:18-21a

Feeding a hungry baby warm milk is deeply gratifying. As our
frantic child slowly relaxes, eyes widening with pleasure,
we're grateful that what we give is so satisfying. What spiritual food our child needs is less obvious. Spiritual nourishment
tends to be overlooked because it's not doled out in ounces.
Yet without it, all the rest that we give will leave our baby
malnourished. Our baby's cries for milk serve as a reminder to
begin regular patterns of spiritual nourishment that flow in the
natural rhythms of the day.

Morning, noon, and night God's goodness comes to us. Raising a word of thanks for it can be as natural as breathing. On rising, we can briefly kneel or throw wide the curtain to welcome the Spirit. When we feed or rock our child we can imagine ourselves being held by God's everlasting arms. As we work we can repeat words of Scripture. As we lay our child down to sleep we can ask God to bless and protect her. As we draw the curtain in the evening we can light a candle and walk with God back through our day.

Spiritual awareness can become as natural as breathing, but earthbound creatures that we are, we need patterns to remind us to draw near to God. Finding fixed moments and fixed places each day to say, "I'm here God. I am with you in this moment. And my work and my child are yours," will fill our days with God's real presence.

Master of the Universe, may awareness of you with us every moment become the air that we breathe and the food that we eat. May your love penetrate all that we do. Amen.

BLESSED ART THOU

Blessed art Thou O Lord our God
  King of the world who makes the fruit of the tree.

Blessed art Thou O Lord our God
  King of the world whose word makes all things on
  the earth.

Blessed art Thou O Lord our God
  King of the world who brings food out of the earth.

Blessed art Thou O Lord our God
  King of the world who gives clothes to cover our bodies.

Blessed art Thou O Lord our God
  King of the world who makes sweet smelling wood
  and plants.

Blessed art Thou O Lord our God
  King of the world who has kept us alive until now so we
  may find joy in what has just come to us.

Blessed art Thou O Lord our God
  King of the world who has created the wonderful things of
  earth and heaven.

—Hebrew Prayer, found in **Peace on Earth**

. . . .

Loud Lamentation in the Land

. . . .

If any of you put a stumbling block before one of these little ones who believe in me, it would be better for you if a great millstone were hung around your neck and you were thrown into the sea.

—Mark 9:42

It is worth repeating that the most important thing we can do for our child is to love our spouse. Recent studies show that the harmful effects of divorce on children are more profound and longer lasting than earlier imagined. Countless children undergo severe suffering because of their parents' inability to truly love each other. When a child's most basic cradle of security is shattered he must struggle to find another safe haven from the terrors that threaten. Usually he fails to find any adequate substitute for that irreplaceable relationship.

It is a child who once again leads us to renew our commitments. The birth of a child brings with it a moral obligation to faithfully love and honor each other for better or worse. By not doing so, we severely endanger our child's well-being. And God who cares especially for children minces no words about those who cause a child to stumble.

But love won't thrive if we only live in fear of judgment. A couple who feel trapped in a destructive relationship can't provide well for a child's security either. When there is abuse and breakdown, it is by the grace of God that we are able nevertheless to provide for our child.

A loving, wholesome relationship often seems impossible to maintain. Yet its worth is beyond price, both for our children and for those of us who learn new lessons in love's power and beauty despite—and often because of—hard times. If we truly love our child, we will devote ourselves daily to love our spouse with body, word and deed.

Holy Lord, preserve us from ever putting our child in jeopardy by our inability to love each other. May we find the help we need in hard times to work out our differences so our commitment to each other will only grow stronger—for our sake and for our precious child. Amen.

FORGIVENESS

Personally, I find it inconceivable that two disciples of Jesus—in this case, joined in marriage—can "walk in the light" and have fellowship unless there is full confession and forgiveness. Confession for the Christian is not merely a spiritual discipline, but a grace: "If we walk in the light, as he is in the light, we have fellowship with one another, and the blood of Jesus, his Son, purifies us from all sin" (1 John 1:7). Because marriage is the most intimate of human relationships, there are daily opportunities to wound and therefore daily opportunities to practice the discipline of confession. . . .

By confession, we have everything to gain and nothing to lose but our self-righteousness. This kind of brokenness can make our marriage whole, especially if it is met with forgiveness. . . .

God meets the couple in the act of forgiveness. (Jean) Vanier asserts that the life of a married couple "is founded on this forgiveness which alone can heal the wounds inflicted on their unity. The road to unity must pass through daily forgiveness. And celebration, which is a sign that forgiveness is total, culminates in the tenderness and union of love. This union of love in spirit and body drives out all aggression and the blockages which might remain, and makes the two one flesh, one heart, one spirit." Then in his most daring metaphor, Vanier suggests that as a couple matures in confession and forgiveness, the sexual embrace is the communion service. "The union becomes eucharistic, an act of thanksgiving for having refound unity."

In the grace of confession and forgiveness we can truly say, "This is my body broken for you," and hear Christ say the same to us.

—*Paul Stevens*, Marriage Spirituality

Cosmic Consequences

Then I saw a new heaven and a new earth; for the first heaven and the first earth had passed away and the sea was no more. . . . And the one who was seated on the throne said, "See, I am making all things new."

—Revelation 21:1, 5a

We are intrigued with the cosmic dimensions of life at home—the early cradling and reliable response to our children's cries that shape their basic ability to trust; their sense of what mother means, what father means, how that forms their first inklings of God; their early intimations of the meaning of covenanted love, a love everlasting no matter what.

Those are some familiar spiritual lessons taught by everyday life. But what about spring cleaning? What on earth does spring cleaning have to do with anything?

A great deal, suggests Walter Wangerin in *Little Lamb, Who Made Thee?* The coming of spring, with the earth "shrugging toward rebirth," reminds him of his mother's spring cleaning. She was a priest, he writes, and this was her sacramental ritual.

"My mother kept cleaning, kept reclaiming territory by the act of cleaning it, kept redeeming her children therein." His mother's feats persuaded Wangerin that "everything old and fusty could be eliminated . . . or better yet, the old itself could be the new again."

Because of her priestly toil to make "my infant world a clean, well-lighted place," Wangerin affirms, "now . . . in spite of wretched evidence to the contrary, I continue to trust in the ultimate purity of God's universe. . . . Never, never should children take so cosmic a gift for granted." Within the smallness of our childhood homes, we learn our most profound and indelible ways of seeing and interpreting the world, he says.

Truly all of life is the raw stuff for telling forth God's goodness. We can't divide the spiritual from the practical. We are "amphibious beings." It is through all the stuff of our ordinary lives that we are fed and can feed our children supernatural food.

May we never underestimate, Creator God, the spiritual dimensions of our everyday doings. We hope that even the dishes we wash, the baths we take, and the beds we prepare teach our children that you are good and they can be confident adventurers. Amen.

(*TM*, April 12, 1994)

GET A GLORY

O you gotta get a glory
    In the work you do,
A Hallelujah chorus
    In the heart of you.
Paint or tell a story,
    Sing or shovel coal,
But you gotta get a glory
    Or the job lacks soul.

—*From a black spiritual, in* **Prayers for Children**

. . . .

Godly Maintenance

. . . .

His master said to him, "Well done, good and trustworthy slave; you have been trustworthy in a few things,
I will put you in charge of many things; enter into the joy
of your master."

—Matthew 25:21

As parents we have a lot more respect for so-called maintenance men and women than we used to. Those of us
who work at teaching or writing often lose touch with what it
really takes to stay warm in the winter, to keep basic systems
functioning, to produce food, to maintain an acceptable level
of cleanliness. Whether it's a school, an office complex, a hospital, or a home, unless the simplest tasks of maintenance are
faithfully looked after, the quality of life quickly deteriorates.

Parenting is a maintenance job. Every day we fight our way
through a veritable jungle of interferences simply to keep the
path to life open for ourselves and our children: picking up,
putting away, wiping up, tying, washing, mixing, feeding,
bandaging . . .

Ernest Boyer Jr. in *Finding God at Home* observes that it is "the very ordinariness of the tasks done day after day that most wear one down, burdening one with fatigue, drudgery, and boredom." But, he suggests, it is possible to perform the ordinary, repetitive acts of the day and find them not meaningless but expressions of a sacred truth. Everything we do can become sacred, he says; it can become fresh and new and beautiful because it is done for God. "God is always present to us," he writes. "The greatest thing we can do in life is to teach ourselves to be always present to God."

Holy One, somehow there is nothing more encouraging than to realize that everything we do is potentially a pathway to you. Teach us to be present to you even in the many mundane things we must do everyday. Amen.

(*TM*, April 13, 1993)

WATCH, THEREFORE

"Watch, therefore." For life in time is not a stumbling from one ecstatic epiphany to another. The enormous task is to keep your eyes open, your wick trimmed, your lamp filled, your powder dry. Even when the bridegroom tarries. Even when the sky falls into the pond and the pond itself is sucked down some sewer of time that comes to nothing. Even when it all flattens out to triviality. Or the midnight cry, "Behold, the bridegroom cometh!" will catch you sleeping, your lamp overturned, the oil spilled out.

And then it is better if you had never been born. The moment you've been waiting for, the end for which you were made—your time—flies without you. Instead of going out to meet the bridegroom, glorious and infinitely desirable, you're in town haggling with the oil dealers. Life himself passes you by. The light dies out. The pond turns its back, closes the door. Depart. It doesn't know you anymore.

There are no two ways about it. You've got your eyes open or you don't. You're watching at midnight or you're not. You must be ready when it comes flying at you, skimming swiftly over the surface of time.

The cares of this world are no excuse. Not father, mother, wife, nor children. Not burials or births or weddings. Not fixing formula, scrubbing the toilet, peddling pills or prose. Whatever the great human enterprise currently in hand, the point is to watch. All the rest is addenda. Seeking the kingdom is the essential integer.

Keep your eyes open or you might as well be dead. You already are.

—*Virginia Stem Owens,*
  And the Trees Clap Their Hands

Loving Father

From ages past no one has heard, no ear has perceived, no eye has seen any God besides you, who works for those who wait for him. . . . Yet, O LORD, you are our Father; we are the clay, and you are our potter; we are all the work of your hand. Do not be exceedingly angry, O LORD, and do not remember our iniquity forever.

—Isaiah 64:4, 8-9a

Isaiah, our ancient ancestor, cries out to God with a stubborn faith. Oh, that you would rend the heavens and come down like you used to. This is not a cry to a distant deity, a force that set the universe in motion and then drifted away. Nor is it a cry to a nature god, a spirit of trees or cliffs. No. This is a cry to one who *acts* on behalf of those who wait. It is a request to one known as "father" and as "potter" who makes us what we are.

And for that very reason, pleads Isaiah, because you father us and shape us into a work of art, because you are that kind of God—don't be angry beyond measure. Come near to us and save us.

It must have felt daringly presumptuous to claim a family connection with the transcendent God of the heavens, and yet what more liberating claim could there be. That Isaiah would appeal to God, because of your *fathering* don't be angry beyond measure but come near, speaks not of a father who is an absent, autocratic unfeeling lord, but one who shows tender care for the well-being of children.

That God as father would care for children—sheltering, feeding, shaping them—provided a model of fatherhood for the Israelites and for all fathers. That the God of Israel would become known as a father God elevated father-love to what it is meant to be—nurturing, guiding, liberating.

Abba, the task of fathering is one in which so many of us fail. Be merciful to us. May fathering in our family be a model of self-giving, daring love and undying devotion. Amen.

(*CH*, pp. 86–88)

INSPECTION

It is written that we shall "stand before" Him, shall appear, shall be inspected. The promise of glory is the promise, almost incredible and only possible by the work of Christ, that some of us, that any of us who really chooses, shall actually survive that examination, shall find approval, shall please God. To please God . . . to be a real ingredient in the divine happiness . . . to be loved by God, not merely pitied, but delighted in as an artist delights in his work or a father in a son—it seems impossible, a weight or burden of glory which our thoughts can hardly sustain. But so it is.

—C. S. *Lewis*, The Weight of Glory

. . . .

Our Story and God's Story

. . . .

Hannah said about her son, Samuel, "For this child I prayed; and the LORD has granted me the petition that I made to him. Therefore I have lent him to the LORD; as long as he lives, he is given to the LORD."

—1 Samuel 1:27-28

The story of Hannah and Elkanah in 1 Samuel is an intriguing one. When Hannah was unable to conceive, Elkanah didn't berate her. Rather, Elkanah comforted her, saying, "Hannah, why do you weep? Why do you not eat? Why is your heart sad? Am I not more to you than ten sons?" It seems Elkanah genuinely cared for Hannah as a person, not only about whether or not she could bear a son.

It is also remarkable that Hannah on her own volition offered any son that they would conceive back to God. There is no evidence that she asked Elkanah's permission or that he objected when she did indeed follow through with giving their child up for the Lord's service. Instead he agreed with her sense of timing about when to take Samuel to Shiloh and joined with her in sacrificial worship on the occasion of Samuel's arrival at the temple of the Lord. The two seem united in devotion to the Lord, marked by regular worship in the temple. They are also apparently in harmony about offering their son to the Lord.

One of the loveliest realizations for young Christian parents is that our child is not only ours but also belongs to God and to the people of God. Our child's story connects with the Great Story of God's faithfulness to humankind. As Christian parents, we are part of a rich and deep history. Our history is bigger and grander than anything we will concoct in our own short lives. And we, by becoming a part of the people of God and dedicating our child to God, are invited into that wonderful Story of stories.

What a legacy we have for our children. What a treasure trove of stories we have to tell them who we are, where we've come from, where we're going. With Hannah and Elkanah, when we commit our children to God, they enter the grandest adventure in the universe.

God of Hannah and Elkanah, we offer our child back to you to serve you and your church. May this small person grow in strength, be filled with wisdom, and enjoy the favor of God for a lifetime. Amen.

SAVE THEM

Dear, supernal Parent, God of my children, save them!

Even as you returned to the race which used its freedom selfishly, unto its death, even as you sent your only begotten Son to die the death which they deserved, return again and again to my young sons and my daughters. . . . In mercy, please! I fear for them if you do not.

Protect them against the enemies that would kill them. But if they must suffer storms or treachery, turn their suffering to advantage—that it always turn them back to you again.

O Lord, I am begging. I mean this prayer with all my heart.

Make my children humble. Let hurting cause in them a genuine humility. And let their transgressions cause no more harm than a personal hurt—for I know them. They will sin. And I beseech you: for their sinning do not damn them, do not let them die, but rather in hurting make them humble. And then, O merciful Father, accept this humility as repentance and let their repentance find your forgiveness and seize them thereby and hold them close unto your bosom forever and ever.

Save them from the world and from themselves. Amen. I love them, sweet Jesus. Amen.

> —*Walter Wangerin Jr.*, **Little Lamb, Who Made Thee?**

. . . .

Imitators of Christ

. . . .

Finally, beloved, whatever is true, whatever is honorable, whatever is just, whatever is pure, whatever is pleasing, whatever is commendable, if there is any excellence and if there is anything worthy of praise, think about these things.

—Philippians 4:8

It's a frightening thought that in many ways our children will imitate us. Oh, you can still get away with a lot when the baby is tiny and unnoticing. But from day one we are observed and imitated whether we like it or not. We remember when words we said in anger suddenly seemed inappropriate; when remarks we were tempted to make about other people needed to be checked lest they be repeated. Our desire for our children to grow up to be generous, polite, truthful, respectful suddenly seemed to hinge largely on whether or not *we* were walking examples of what we wanted them to become.

Are we parents persons of integrity? It's a question we often try to discern prayerfully. We find that our children, more than anyone, keep us accountable.

They see us up front preaching on a Sunday. But they also see us grouchy in the morning and angry when pushed too far. They see how we spend our money and what we say about people behind their backs. They know how we pray and what we think of prayer. They know whether we honestly admit our failures and ask forgiveness.

If what we say we believe and how we behave ring true, they may decide that the way we've chosen to walk can be trusted to serve them well too. If they see too many inconsistencies and can't find a common thread of integrity, they may look for another way. It's a challenge—being real people who have an honest, unsentimentalized faith, a faith that directly impacts the way we live each day. We hope, with the grace of God and forgiving grace of our children and friends, to live with integrity.

Jesus, we make bold to ask that our child will be an imitator of us as we are an imitator of Christ. We want our lives to be worthy of you and for our child to choose you because our lives ring true. Amen.

(*TM*, February 8, 1994)

CONFESSION

Confession is so difficult a Discipline for us partly because we view the believing community as a fellowship of saints before we see it as a fellowship of sinners. We come to feel that everyone else has advanced so far into holiness that we are isolated and alone in our sin. We could not bear to reveal our failures and shortcomings to others. We imagine that we are the only ones who have not stepped onto the high road to heaven. Therefore we hide ourselves from one another and live in veiled lies and hypocrisy.

But if we know that the people of God are first a fellowship of sinners we are freed to hear the unconditional call of God's love and to confess our need openly before our brothers and sisters. We know we are not alone in our sin. The fear and pride which cling to us like barnacles cling to others also. We are sinners together. In acts of mutual confession we release the power that heals. Our humanity is no longer denied but transformed.

—Richard J. Foster, **Celebration of Discipline**

. . . .

Where Joy and Pain Converge

. . . .

It is by your holding fast to the word of life that I can boast on the day of Christ that I did not run in vain or labor in vain. But even if I am being poured out as a libation over the sacrifice and the offering of your faith, I am glad and rejoice with all of you.

—Philippians 2:16-17

In a conversation with a friend, Sara learned that he and his wife were expecting their first baby. They shared the thrill, tingling together with the awareness of what a momentous event this is for parents-to-be.

Then Sara said, "And be prepared to have your heart torn out."

He gulped. His eyes said, Did you have to say that now?

The timing was bad. But for us, opening our hearts to love a child meant opening them to joy and pain beyond belief. When our child is hurt in any way, we hurt. When he suffers, we do. When he has a great day, we shout hallelujahs. We live constantly on the edge—a precarious balancing of the good and the difficult. We live in constant hope that the good is sufficient to sustain us through the hard times. Sometimes it barely reaches.

Someone has said that our capacity for joy is carved out by the degree of pain we have known. There is an intimate relationship between the two beyond what we can explore here. But there are at least two things we have learned about their dynamic convergence in our parenting. First, the less afraid we are of our own pain and failure, the more we know joy and can freely and honestly give ourselves to our children.

Second, in our chosen vocation, parenting, joy and pain converge with an intensity that often leaves us wishing we'd chosen something more mundane. But then the life of faith means being willing to risk everything for love's sake. And parenting, as painful as it sometimes seems, is a supreme joy.

Merciful One, somehow our intimate relationships at home open us to more joy and pain than anything else. We commit ourselves to nurture those closest to us despite the risk, because there's nothing we'd rather do than enlarge the circle of love. Amen.

(*TM*, October 12, 1993)

THE SINGING OF ANGELS

There must be always remaining in every man's life some place for the singing of angels, some place for that which in itself is breathlessly beautiful and, by an inherent prerogative, throws all the rest of life into a new and creative relatedness, something that gathers up in itself all the freshets of experience from drab and commonplace areas of living and glows in one bright white light of penetrating beauty and meaning—then passes. The commonplace is shot through with new glory; old burdens become lighter; deep and ancient wounds lose much of their old, old hurting. A crown is placed over our heads that for the rest of our lives we are trying to grow tall enough to wear. Despite all the crassness of life, despite all the hardness of life, despite all the harsh discords of life, life is saved by the singing of angels.

—*Howard Thurman*, **Deep Is the Hunger**[6]

·················

Endnotes

················

Some meditations included in this book have been adapted from earlier writings by Sara Wenger Shenk. Meditations marked *AT* are adapted from *And Then There Were Three*, © 1985 by Herald Press. Used by permission of Herald Press; *CH* from *Coming Home*, © 1992 by Good Books. Used by permission of Good Books; *TM* from Sara's columns in *The Mennonite*.

The publisher attempted to trace the ownership of all poems and quotations and to secure all necessary permissions from authors or holders of copyrights. Should there be any oversight in making proper acknowledgment, upon notification the publisher will correct such omissions in any future editions of this publication.

For reprint use of copyrighted works, the author and publisher are indebted to the sources listed below.

1. Ernest Boyer Jr., *Finding God at Home*, Harper & Row, 1988. © 1984 by Ernest Boyer Jr. Used by permission.
2. Walter Wangerin Jr., *Little Lamb, Who Made Thee?* Zondervan Publishing House. © 1993 by Walter Wangerin Jr. Used by permission of Zondervan Publishing House.

3. Howard Thurman, *The Inward Journey*. © 1961 by Harper & Row.

4. Richard Gillard, "The Servant Song." © 1977 by Scripture in Song, a division of Integrity Music. Administered by Maranatha! Music, c/o The Copyright Company, Nashville, TN. All rights reserved. International copyright secured. Used by permission.

5. Henri J. M. Nouwen, *Out of Solitude*, Ave Maria Press, 1974. © 1974 by Ave Maria Press, Notre Dame, IN 46556. All rights reserved. Used by permission of the publisher.

6. Howard Thurman, *Deep Is the Hunger*. © 1951 by Harper & Row.

The Authors

Gerald and Sara Wenger Shenk are both lifelong writers and trained educators with doctoral degrees, and were quickly smitten with a rich and abiding love as their three "cherubs" (now adults) were born. Sara is president of Anabaptist Mennonite Biblical Seminary in Elkhart Indiana, and previously taught at Eastern Mennonite Seminary for fifteen years. Gerald taught  at EMS for twenty-one years and now serves as a development officer, with occasional teaching. Both have been published extensively; Sara is the author of several additional books on parenting and family life. Sara and Gerald and their three children spent their early family years in the former Yugoslavia, where Gerald and Sara worked with local churches and theological education under assignment by Mennonite Central Committee and Eastern Mennonite Missions. Those early family years in a cross-cultural setting prompted much reflection on the significance of parenting.

THE HERALD PRESS MEDITATION BOOKS
OVER HALF A MILLION COPIES IN PRINT.

"Attractively packaged and pleasant."
—*Christian Century*

"This series has been around for a number of years
. . . and captures the spirit of Christian love."
—*Christian Citizen*

"Attractive enough for a Christmas gift
and cherishable any month of the year."
—*The Christian Reader*

Available January 2015

Available Fall 2015